FRED BASSET YEARBOOK 2021



Drawings by Michael Martin





An Hachette UK Company
www.hachette.co.uk

Summersdale Publishers Ltd
Part of Octopus Publishing Group Limited
Carmelite House
50 Victoria Embankment
LONDON
EC4Y 0DZ
UK

www.summersdale.com

Printed and bound in the UK

ISBN: 978-1-78783-553-5

DO YOU FANCY A STROLL THROUGH THE PARK WITH FRED, DEAR ?
YES, LET'S. WE CAN TAKE HIS BALL !
My thoughts exactly !!
We're having an in-depth chat with Jock —
YAP YAP YAPPITY YAP YAP YAP
It's a little one-sided...
YAP YAP

I spy my choc-drops!
And look — They still have plenty of shelf life!
Or at least they did have!!
MGM

COME ON, FRED — OFF MY CHAIR!
I am using the old 'I'm fast asleep, please don't disturb me' ploy –
ZZZZZZ
A ploy, I fear, I may have over-used...
ZZZZZZ
A ploy, I fear, that may be wearing rather thin!
ZZZZZZ
MGM

Jock ? Yorky ?
I wonder where they're off to ?
Into the unknown !
Create a password ?
number1fred ?
But surely everyone knows that ?!

She's trying out her new hat for the wedding tomorrow—
IT LOOKS WONDERFUL, DEAR!
He's being very diplomatic!
There are no boy job/girl jobs around here!
M&M
M&M

WOOF WOOF
YAP YAP
It's nice to receive a bit of positive feedback!
YAPPITY YAP
MRM

Road rage ?!
MRM
OH, CHARLIE— DO STOP IT!

I know it might only be mid-morning, lads —
But I'm calling it a day!
For a moment there I was lost for words!

THEY LOOK HELPFUL, DEAR!
MMM...
Where's the snow?!
M&M
Calm down, lads—
YIP
YIP
YIP
YAP
YAP
YAP
Share and share alike!
M&M

He's home!
Just what I need—
A man hug!
MSM
For the sake of health and safety—
I shall refrain from sitting in the front row!
MSM

Enter stage left —
FRED HAS BEEN DIGGING IN THE VEGETABLE PATCH AGAIN — I'LL GIVE HIM A TICKING OFF WHEN I SEE HIM!
Exit stage right!!
We're going to the beach!
We haven't been for ages!
Long time no sea!!

Uh oh—This chap looks a bit suspicious!
Jock, Yorky, Taffy, Bruce!
Safety in numbers!
After a delicious meal—
FRED
What more could I ask for?!

WOOF WOOF
WOOF
Answer came there none!
L.O.L.!
Laugh Out Loud!!

DING DONG
OH GREAT—THANK YOU VERY MUCH. 'BYE!
PIZZA, LADS!
Do I qualify as one of the lads?!

Oh, Yorky, you've let the side down!
That's what cats do!!

What a day I've had—
I'm exhausted!
FRED—OFF MY CHAIR, NOW!
Now?
Now is not a good time!
Would you mind if I helped myself to a drink, Jock?
A wee dram is all I'm after!
JOCK

Mrs. Jones has left some sausages out on her kitchen table!
Nobody knows what goes on behind closed doors!
M&M

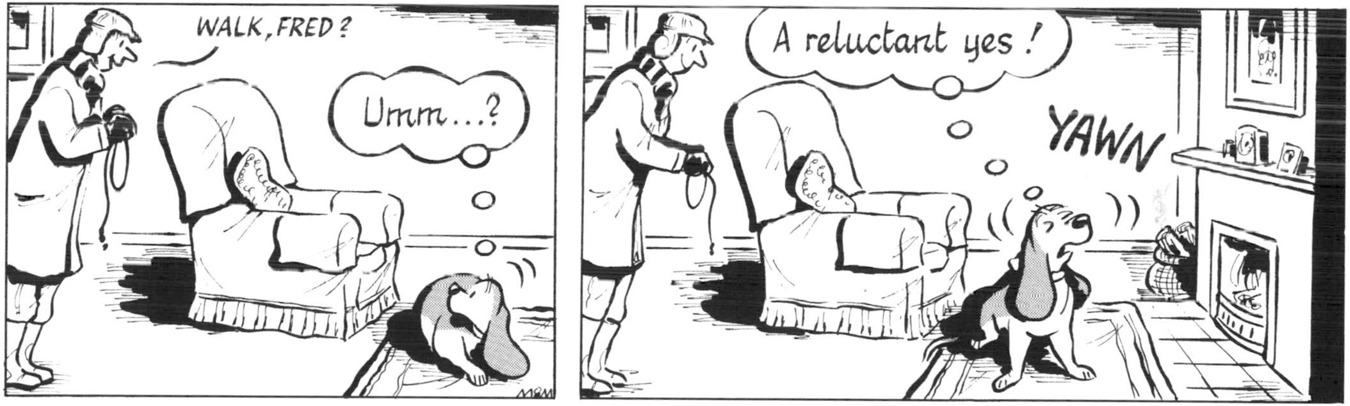
WALK, FRED?
Umm...?
M&M
A reluctant yes!
YAWN

I think I'll take the middle ground!

Take-away leftovers!
FRED
Wow— Spicy!
That packs a punch!
FRED

A bit of toast!
A crisp or two!
A chocolate biscuit!
Grazing!

I am outside my comfort zone —
This is more like it!

Yorky—
Show 'em what you're made of!
M&M
CAREFUL, FRED!
Why?!
WEAK BRIDGE
M&M

We live in a democracy, lads—Free speech and all that...
...of course you can all have your say...
...as long as you remember that it's me who has the **last** say!!
MSM
SEE YOU LATER, DEAR!
Off he goes—
MSM
SEE YOU LATER, FRED!
Off she goes—
Doggy Doldrums!

Well — We're not going to stand for that sort of behaviour, are we, lads?
All together now —
MGM
IT LOOKS A BIT WINDY FOR A WALK, FRED...
...AND LOOK AT THOSE CLOUDS COMING OVER!
I THOUGHT SO — IT'S STARTING TO RAIN!
For goodness' sake, man up!
MGM

A new delivery of sausages at the butchers?
Thanks for the tip-off!!
MSM

I would like a walk and I would like it right now...
...and I am not taking no for an answer!!
MSM

Unflappable!
TWEET
MBM

The best thing about a long-term relationship is —
Togetherness!
MBM

Do you mind ?! This is a top-secret meeting –
YAP WOOF WOOF
YAP YAP Yip Yap
Yip Yap
YAP Yip Yip Yap
Sorted !
M&M

This may be keeping him fit...
...but there's not much fresh air involved !
M&M

Scruffy?
Canine Salon
He has been reinvented!
OH, HE'S JUST ADORABLE!
Her sister in Australia has a new kitten—
ME-OW
So near yet so far!!
WOOF
WOOF
WOOF
FOR GOODNESS' SAKE, FRED!
WOOF
WOOF

You wouldn't get me up in one of those things—
Even with an engine!!
MSM
Ah, there he is—
He and me time!
MSM

What's up, Yorky?
Stop whimpering — Go back and sort things out!
You're made of sterner stuff than that!!
Ready, lads?
Let's party!
Happy Birthday Amanda

DON'T YOU DARE COME IN HERE WITH MUDDY FEET!
The powers that be have spoken!

IT WAS LOVELY TO SEE STEPHEN AND DENISE, WASN'T IT?
YES—SHAME ABOUT HIS TROUSERS, THOUGH!
I KNOW—HOW EMBARRASSING, I DIDN'T REALISE FRED WAS SO MUDDY!
I jumped up to greet him!
AND DENISE'S NEW DRESS!
I jumped up to greet her too!

I THOUGHT YOU WERE SORTING OUT THE SHED, DEAR?
I HAVE!
Into an organised mess?!
M&M

READY, FRED?
I'm feeling a bit under the weather, but I guess I'm ready–
The show must go on, and all that...
M&M

F.B.
F.B.
Brand Fred Basset!
F.B.
MGM

I love this tune!
MGM
Or at least I did!!

FORD
No prizes for guessing who will be testing the depth !
M&M

YAWN
M&M

There's nothing like an impromptu performance from Jock to liven up the day !
Yappity Yap
Yappity Yap

When the going gets tough—
Whimper !
The path ahead is looking rather daunting—
M&M
M&M

The diet isn't going too well –
He's a lost cause!
Good morning!
Are you by any chance taking a stroll around the park?
Would you mind if I joined you?
My new best friend!

FRED!!
Success!
Short-lived!
'MORNING, FRED! WAKEY WAKEY!
Not yet, pleeeease...
Just another five minutes?!

Yorky's a wannabe —
YIP YIP YIPPITY YIP
MGM
I am not surprised you are feeling a bit peaky, Yorky !
Downing six jumbo sausages is more than enough for anyone !!
MGM

DOGGY BIX
FRED
M&M
He has stopped?
I didn't say when!!
DOGGY BIX
FRED
COME ON, FRED—LET'S GET HOME QUICKLY!
THAT STORM IS CLOSING IN FAST!
Batten down the hatches!
M&M

SHALL WE?
Yes, let's!
A golden opportunity, I reckon!
The Golden Duck
Menu
Special Offer 2 for 1 meals
MSM

WHAT ON EARTH IS GOING ON?!
A big dig!
MSM

It sounds as if Jock is in trouble with those wretched terriers again!
YAP
YAP
A friend in need is a friend indeed —
OFF you go, lads!
M&M
HERE COMES FUNNY FRED!
COME ON FUNNY FRED — GET A MOVE ON! YOU CAN DO IT!!
There seem to be Freds everywhere these days!
GO FOR IT!
... IN THE LAST FURLONG IT'S FUNNY FRED LEADING BY A HEAD...
M&M

That's very kind of you, mate!
I'm a very lucky chap to have a friend like Jock helping me out with burying my bone—
Although I wouldn't put it past said friend to have an ulterior motive!
M&M

ARE YOU COMING UP HERE, FRED?
No thanks!
HOW ABOUT HERE, FRED?
No thanks!
Nothing personal!
M&M

YAP YIP YAP YAP
YAP YAP YIP
YAP YIP
A safe pair of hands!
YAP YIP YAP YAP
YIP
MSM
With my drive, tenacity and leadership qualities, we can achieve anything, lads –
MSM
Can't we ?!

IT WASN'T OUR FAULT!
They would say that, wouldn't they?!
HERE'S YOUR DINNER, FRED!
But I've had it already!
FRED
EAT IT UP, FRED!
She obviously didn't tell him before she went out!
FRED
The lack of communication in this household does have its advantages!
FRED
M&M

WHAT ON EARTH ARE YOU UP TO, FRED?!
Nothing?

Here he comes!
He was in there somewhere, wasn't he?!

OH, FRED — FOR GOODNESS' SAKE!
Why is it always *my* fault?!
BE CAREFUL, LADS!
SORRY — FRED WAS IN THE WAY AND I TRIPPED OVER HIM!
He should know never to work with children and animals!

On your marks —
Get set —
Gone !!
HERE, FRED !
Sorry, I can't right now —
I have a lot on my mind —

Oh good — The Tucker Twins have been safely rounded up —
YIPPEEEE!
Sausages!
FRED!!
You could say I have a perchant for them!

My best bone –
Bar none !!

Make way –
Basset boarding –
Ready for take-off !

In case Jock has a mishap...
...his understudy is waiting in the wings!
M&M

BERT IS A NIGHTMARE IN THE GARDEN!
FRED IS EXACTLY THE SAME!
ONLY THE OTHER DAY FRED DUG UP MY VEGETABLE PATCH — WHAT A MESS HE MADE!!
BERT DUG UP ALL MY DAHLIAS!
FRED CHASED A CAT THROUGH THE ROSES!
Why can't they just accept us for what we are, Bert?!
M&M

Option 1— Jump ?
Option 2— Swim ?
Option 3 it is !!
MSM

She's out for the evening with Angela !
Luckily he has the basic survival skills—
Just !
MSM

Uh oh!
I had better be on my best behaviour!
HELLO, BERT!
BERT—BERT BASSET!
Misnomer, mate!

Front gate shut –
Side gate shut –
Landlocked!!
MGM

COME ON, FRED!
GOOD BOY, FRED!
TROT ON, FRED!
I'm assuming she's talking to me?!
MGM

GET OUT FROM UNDER MY FEET, FRED — YOU'RE NOTHING BUT A NUISANCE!
GET OFF THE VEGETABLE PATCH, FRED — YOU NAUGHTY BOY!
At least someone is pleased to see me!
TWEET TWEET TWEET
MGM
As they are out for the afternoon, I shall treat myself to an upgrade —
MGM

FIRST YOU WANT OUT AND THEN YOU WANT IN— FOR GOODNESS' SAKE, MAKE UP YOUR MIND!
He could always install a **Fred**-flap!

COME ALONG, FRED!
Uh oh!
Don't look down, Fred— Don't look down, Fred— Don't look down, Fred—

WOULD YOU LIKE YOUR DINNER, FRED?
BE A GOOD BOY AND PASS ME YOUR BOWL, THEN!
FRED
Yes, chef!
FRED
M&M

COME ON, FRED!
His new trainers are proving to be rather too comfortable –
KEEP UP, FRED!
Our normal stroll through the park has turned into a route march!!
M&M

She likes everything spick and span!
Including me!

OH LOOK, ALBERT, HOW SWEET!
I am a people magnet!
HE'S A HANDSOME CHAP!
MUM, DOGGY!
WHAT A GOOD BOY!
CAN I STROKE THE DOGGY, MUMMY?
OH DADDY, HE'S LOVELY!

It's nothing personal, Jock ...
... but Jemma wishes to stroll around the park with me!
Oh!
Let's just wait for the wind to change direction!

Oh, hello –
Huntley Manor
Gardens
Show off !

WHAT ARE YOU UP TO, FRED ?
Doodling !

Is anyone up for a walk?
Nope, by the look of things!

READY, FRED?
Nope!
STEADY, FRED?
Nope!
GO, FRED?
Nope!

Virtual reality ?
It looks like real reality to me!!
WHO WOULD LIKE A CHOC-DROP, THEN?!
It's a shame this isn't a waggy tail competition —
I reckon I'd be the outright winner!

Uh oh — Mrs. Johnson's ginger tom!
I shall tiptoe by gingerly!

So, Jock, you reckon that Scruffy looks a bit off-colour?
How can you tell?!

I have been volunteered to retrieve our ball —
WHAT ON EARTH ?!
Wish me luck !
SLOW UP A BIT, FRED !
You'd think it would be me trying to keep up with him —
He's the one on the vitamin supplements !

Yorky !
He got more than he bargained for !
MGM

Nail Salon
Nail Salon
My turn ?
MGM

YIP YIP YIP
Jock ?
YAP YAP YAP
Well, I think it's Jock—
YIP YIP YIP YAP YAP YAP
Some days I can't tell his *yip* from his *yap* !
MOM
I WONDER WHY THAT CAT RACED ACROSS THE LAWN LIKE THAT ?
Wonder not !
MOM

I'll be right out, lads!
Come on — Hurry up!
I can't contain my excitement much longer!
M&M

I HAVE JUST DOWNLOADED THESE LOVELY PHOTOGRAPHS I TOOK OF FRED, DEAR!
Mmm...
Is there an airbrushing facility?!
M&M

From a few bumbling tricks in the back garden to this —
Jock's meteoric rise to stardom!
CHURCH FÊTE

Is that what is called creative block?!

Encore ?!

YAY !
Yay !

Jock has stolen your bone and he won't give it back ?!
There, there, Yorky — I know the feeling !

Happy Birthday Mia
I DO HOPE THE CHILDREN DON'T MAKE A MESS WITH THE FOOD !
Don't worry about that, dear —
We've got it covered !

Now we've had our main course ...
FRED
JOCK
YORKY
... we're moving on to our sweets !
CHOC-DROP, LADS ?
MGM
We're having a great time —
My sidekick and I !
MGM

Oooh— Goody! A bit of bacon rind!
Gone ??
In one fell swoop !!
MGM
FETCH, FRED!
THE BALL, FRED—FETCH!!
FRED—FETCH THE BALL!
Sorry— I'm just not in the zone!
MGM

DINNER, FRED!
HERE YOU ARE!
But he has already fed me!
FRED
Who am I to complain?!
FRED
I should have known better!

Ha-ha
No, I'm **not** laughing, Yorky—
It really **is** a ha-ha!
Some days things can really get on top of me—
But hey-ho...!
YIP YAP — YIP YAP
YIP YAP
YIP YAP
MSM

Banished to the sidelines!
Apparently chasing the jack is not an option!

WHAT DO YOU FANCY FOR DINNER TODAY THEN, FRED?
FRED
TUNA AND SALMON? DUCK AND VEGETABLE? STEAK AND KIDNEY?
FRED
All the above!

AREN'T YOU GOING TO BRUSH FRED BEFORE YOU TAKE HIS PICTURE?
Don't fuss, dear —
He can airbrush me later!
HE LOOKS FINE — SMILE, FRED!

Yorky has always been good at football —
But today, he's definitely on top of his game!

Things have come to a head —
Head to head !!

PHEW — THIS CROSSWORD IS WELL NIGH IMPOSSIBLE !
Come on, man — Use that brain of yours !
If you don't use it you'll lose it !

If you look up to me, lads, you can tell which way the wind is blowing —
N
E
S
W
M&M

GOOD BOY, FRED!
This is the last time!
M&M
If he chooses to wallop it into the bushes again, then he can get it himself!
DO BE GENTLE, DEAR!

Banished from the Barrington-Smyths' tea party?!
Your best behaviour, lads—That's all I asked—
Splashing in their pool and helping yourselves to their cupcakes is **not** what I call best behaviour!!
OK, FRED—S.. OH, GOOD BOY!
AND GIVE ME YOUR P.. OH, GOOD BOY!
When a choc-drop is involved, I'm way ahead of him!

I'LL SET UP MY PHONE HERE AND WE CAN TAKE A PICTURE WITH FRED!
Where did he come from?!
CLICK

CONGRATULATIONS, TOM — GREAT GAME, WELL DONE!
Beaten six and five!
WE'LL HAVE TO DO IT AGAIN SOME TIME!
He didn't stand a chance!
YEP — MAYBE AFTER SCHOOL NEXT WEEK?
He hides his humiliation well!

Cucumber sandwiches ? Scones ?
TEA, DEAR ?
MMM... YES PLEASE !
Quintessentially British !
Wait a moment, lads— Before you enter, I must carry out a Health and Safety check—
Yep—It's fine !

Phew–That was close!
ISN'T HE HANDSOME!
YES, HE'S LOVELY!
AND SO CUTE!
Oh stop it, please–
WHO'S A GORGEOUS BOY, THEN...?
If I could, I would blush!

Oh the monotony!
I know–
I spy with my little eye...
HERE YOU ARE, FRED!
The cheek of it!

DO YOU WANT TO JOIN US, FRED?
Huh—You wouldn't get me up in one of those things!
COME ON, FRED!
What I mean is—Physically you wouldn't get me up in one of those things!
Crumbs!
Small pleasures!

I'VE BEEN TALKING WITH ANN ABOUT THE POSSIBILITY OF THE TWINS COMING ON HOLIDAY WITH US—
SHE THINKS IT'S A WONDERFUL IDEA!
Me too!
WHAT DO YOU THINK, DEAR?
Although he needs convincing!
...UM...
OK, BOYS—IT'S A LONG JOURNEY TO THE HOLIDAY PARK, SO LET'S ALL BE PATIENT!
I don't think there will be a problem!

COME ON, FRED!
I'll soon catch them up —
With a little help!
Holiday Park
ANYONE FOR SAUSAGES?
YES, PLEASE!
Need you ask ?!
Holiday Park

Choppy waters ahead—
Boat Hire
Holiday Park
7
M&M

WHEEEEE
That looks fun!
M&M
AAARRGHHHH!
But not for him!

A holiday success!
A wonderful time was had by all!
ZZZZ
When it comes to friends—
Jock and Yorky are my best ones!

READY, LADS?
Yep!
He spoils us!
Yip
Yorky?
We have a stowaway!
Yip Yip
M&M

The hunter-gatherers return!
Jock's new trick!
He didn't quite pull it off!

What a day I've had!
Make way—Coming through—
I need to de-stress!

Whenever we're out and about, Jock always puts on a show of some sort—
YAPPITY YAP
YAP YAP
I call it showing off!
YAPPITY YAP YAP YAP YAP YAP
YAPPITY YAP YAP YAP YAPPITY YAP
YAP
YAP

MAY WE PLAY WITH FRED?
YES—HE WON'T MIND!
Do I have a say in this?!
BRRRMMM
BEEP BEEP

YIP YIP YIP YIP YIP YIP YIP YIP YIP YIP YIP
YAP YAP YAP YAP YAP YAP YAP YAP YAP YAP YAP
YIPPITY YAP YAPPITY YIP YAPPITY YAP YAP YIP YAP
WOOF
I always have the last word!

FR-ED!
I do enjoy a spot of lunch alfresco!
FRED
Yorky — That's far enough —
DO NOT DISTURB!

DO YOU WANT TO GO OUT, FRED?
Yes please!
WOOF
Aren't you coming?!

I've always thought that going for a walk meant going for a walk...
I'm a little bewildered!
OFF WE GO, BUBBLES!

They have their differences—
No more so than when it comes to the matter of scones!
Cream or jam first?!
Cream Teas
Stand back, lads—Let me assess the situation—
Assessed!!

DID YOU HAVE A NICE WALK, DEAR?
YES—LOVELY. FRED CHASED A RABBIT!
HE ALMOST CAUGHT UP WITH IT TOO...
... UNTIL HE TRIPPED OVER HIS EARS!
It's easily done!
ZZZ
WALK, FRED?
Living the dream!

It's a shame he didn't bring his piano—
He could have joined in!
M&M

Uh oh—A toddler. I'm about to get a big pat on the head or a tug on my ears!
DOGGY
COME ALONG, JAMIE!
Phew!
That's a good boy—Toddle off!
MAMA
M&M

Here he comes—
F.B.'s B.F. —
Fred Basset's Best Friend !!
Even after walking for what seems like hours—
They still feel the need to go that extra mile !
SHALL WE ?
The Royal Oak
Real Ales
Good
Home-Made
Food
1 Mile
Dogs welcome

It's that pair of terriers from number twenty-nine on the warpath!
Three against two doesn't seem very fair, lads—
Allow me to even things up a little!

Lunchtime Special 2 for 1 menu
SHALL WE?
Lunchtime Special 2 for 1 menu
MMM...
What about me?!

Urgh !
Oh to be home sweet home !
FRED
He makes a very good maître d' !
ENJOY !
FRED
MSM

I am on a research and development course—
Research—
Development !!
Wake up and smell the coffee !!

HELLO THERE — AND WHAT'S YOUR NAME, THEN?
Sorry — I'm not obliged to answer —
Data protection and all that...
MEM

Ready, lads?
Photobombed!
MEM

Would you like me to lend a hand, Jock?
A paw?
Don't be so pedantic!!
MBM

MBM
Ok, I can take a hint!

DING DONG
DING DONG
DING DONG
DING DONG
They're learning the ropes!
COME ON, FRED — YOU CAN DO IT!
I don't rate my chances!

Hello there!
Lovely day, isn't it?
Are you new to the area?
Somewhat lacking in charisma?!
M&M

We are waiting for Jock to swing into action—
M&M

Guy Fawkes Night—
I go like a rocket!
MGM
Off he goes...
... into his own little world!
MGM

HAPPY ANNIVERSARY, DEAR!
Goodness, he has remembered?
GRAB YOUR COAT, I'VE BOOKED A TABLE AT THE GOURMET TAVERN IN THE HIGH STREET!
Flowers, chocolates and dinner out?!
SEE YOU LATER, FRED!
Wonders will never cease!

OH FRED—DO YOU HAVE TO DO THAT?!
Yep!

MRS. JOHNSON'S CAT IS IN OUR GARDEN AGAIN, FRED!
ARE YOU GOING TO CHASE HIM OFF?
Try stopping me!!

CAREFUL, BOYS — YOU'RE DROPPING YOUR LUNCH ON THE FLOOR!
Fred the canine vacuum cleaner springs into action!

He saw sense !
I like to do my bit !

One of life's little mysteries —
YORKY
Where does he put it ?!
YORKY
Please — My waistline!
Go easy on the carbs!
Doggy Bix
FRED

The first bark of the day—
And it won't be the last!
MGM

Hello everyone!
So nice to see you all!
They are in a world of their own!
MGM

That is the third time he has pressed that snooze button!
He'll be late for work, won't he?
We can't be having that, can we?!

SHALL WE TRY OUT THAT SALSA, DEAR?
This could be fun– Turn up the music and let's see their fancy footwork!
MMM... THAT'S SPICY!
How disappointing!

Come along, lads, it's no longer fit for purpose!
MSM
So far so good—
MSM
He hasn't put a foot wrong!

WE NEED TO NIP OUT TO DO SOME CHRISTMAS SHOPPING, DEAR!
Not for me, thanks!
IF WE STROLL ALONG THE HIGH STREET WE CAN POP INTO THE PET SHOP FOR SOME TREATS FOR FRED!
But then again...
M&M
AAAH—AT LAST, FRED, A BIT OF PEACE AND QUIET!
DING DONG
HELLO, DARLING, WE THOUGHT WE WOULD POP IN TO WISH YOU ALL A VERY HAPPY CHRISTMAS!
YAP YIP YIP YAP YIP YAP YIP YAP YIP YAP YIP YAP YIP YAP YIP YAP YAP YIP
He spoke too soon!
YIP YAP YIP YIP

Such messy guests they are ...
... which suits me down to the ground!
MBM
COME ON, FRED — BEDTIME!
Can I sleep here? Just for tonight??
I have an early start!
MBM

All aboard, lads!
First stop — The food station!
Please alight here and help yourselves!

LOOK OUT, FRED!
There has been an increase in traffic around here since Christmas!
BZZZZ
BZZZZ
BZZZZ

WHAT'S FOR SUPPER THIS EVENING, DEAR?
RISOTTO!
OH, THAT SOUNDS NICE!
The turkey is still going strong!
A LOVELY CLEAN BLANKET, FRED!
I'VE EVEN GIVEN YOUR BUNNY A SPRING CLEAN TOO!
That will do nicely!